Roger Williams

Founder of Rhode Island

Colonial Leaders

Lord Baltimore
English Politician and Colonist

Benjamin Banneker
American Mathematician and Astronomer

Sir William Berkeley
Governor of Virginia

William Bradford
Governor of Plymouth Colony

Jonathan Edwards
Colonial Religious Leader

Benjamin Franklin
American Statesman, Scientist, and Writer

Anne Hutchinson
Religious Leader

Cotton Mather
Author, Clergyman, and Scholar

Increase Mather
Clergyman and Scholar

James Oglethorpe
Humanitarian and Soldier

William Penn
Founder of Democracy

Sir Walter Raleigh
English Explorer and Author

Caesar Rodney
American Patriot

John Smith
English Explorer and Colonist

Miles Standish
Plymouth Colony Leader

Peter Stuyvesant
Dutch Military Leader

George Whitefield
Clergyman and Scholar

Roger Williams
Founder of Rhode Island

John Winthrop
Politician and Statesman

John Peter Zenger
Free Press Advocate

Revolutionary War Leaders

John Adams
Second U.S. President

Ethan Allen
Revolutionary Hero

Benedict Arnold
Traitor to the Cause

King George III
English Monarch

Nathanael Greene
Military Leader

Nathan Hale
Revolutionary Hero

Alexander Hamilton
First U.S. Secretary of the Treasury

John Hancock
President of the Continental Congress

Patrick Henry
American Statesman and Speaker

John Jay
First Chief Justice of the Supreme Court

Thomas Jefferson
Author of the Declaration of Independence

John Paul Jones
Father of the U.S. Navy

Lafayette
French Freedom Fighter

James Madison
Father of the Constitution

Francis Marion
The Swamp Fox

James Monroe
American Statesman

Thomas Paine
Political Writer

Paul Revere
American Patriot

Betsy Ross
American Patriot

George Washington
First U.S. President

Famous Figures of the Civil War Era

Jefferson Davis
Confederate President

Frederick Douglass
Abolitionist and Author

Ulysses S. Grant
Military Leader and President

Stonewall Jackson
Confederate General

Robert E. Lee
Confederate General

Abraham Lincoln
Civil War President

William Sherman
Union General

Harriet Beecher Stowe
Author of Uncle Tom's Cabin

Sojourner Truth
Abolitionist, Suffragist, and Preacher

Harriet Tubman
Leader of the Underground Railroad

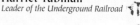

Roger Williams

Founder of Rhode Island

Amy Allison

Arthur M. Schlesinger, jr.
Senior Consulting Editor

Publishers

Philadelphia

Produced by Pre-Press Company, Inc., East Bridgewater, MA 02333

CHELSEA HOUSE PUBLISHERS
Editor in Chief Stephen Reginald
Production Manager Pamela Loos
Art Director Sara Davis
Director of Photography Judy L. Hasday
Managing Editor James D. Gallagher
Senior Production Editor J. Christopher Higgins

Staff for *ROGER WILLIAMS*
Project Editor Anne Hill
Associate Art Director Takeshi Takahashi
Series Design Keith Trego

The Chelsea House World Wide Web address is http://www.chelseahouse.com

First Printing
1 3 5 7 9 8 6 4 2

Library of Congress Cataloging-in-Publication Data

Allison, Amy, 1956–
    Roger Williams / Amy Allison.
        p. cm. — (Colonial leaders)
    Includes bibliographical references and index.
    ISBN 0-7910-5964-2 (HC); 0-7910-6121-3 (PB)
    1. Williams, Roger, 1604?–1683—Juvenile literature. 2. Puritans—
Rhode Island—Biography—Juvenile literature. 3. Baptists—Rhode Island—
Biography—Juvenile literature. 4. Separatists—Rhode Island—Biography—
Juvenile literature. 5. Pioneers—Rhode Island—Biography—Juvenile
literature 6. Providence (R.I.)—History—17th century—Juvenile literature.
7. Rhode Island—History—Colonial period, ca. 1600–1775—Juvenile
literature. [1. Williams, Roger, 1604?–1683. 2. United States—History—
Colonial period, ca. 1600–1775—Biography. 3. Reformers.] I. Title. II. Series.

F82.W7 A45 2000
974.5'02'092—dc21
[B]   00-038387

Publisher's Note: In Colonial and Revolutionary War America, there were no standard rules for spelling, punctuation, capitalization, or grammar. Some of the quotations that appear in the Colonial Leaders and Revolutionary War Leaders series come from original documents and letters written during this time in history. Original quotations reflect writing inconsistencies of the period.

Contents

The Williams family had a thriving cloth business on Cow Lane in London. In the shop in the front of the family home, James Williams and his sons sold costly materials to the wealthy customers that hurried about the business district.

1

A Hopeful Lad

Bells filled the air with the news: England had a new king. *What would life be like without good Queen Bess?* people wondered. *Would there be the same peace and plenty under King James?*

The year 1603 brought more reason to worry. A deadly disease, the bubonic plague, swept through the city of London. No one knew for sure what caused it or how to stop it. The rats that carried the disease ran freely through the streets. Thousands died. One family buried 10 children.

The Williams family was lucky. Both newborn Roger and his older brother, Sydrach, survived.

They could escape the cramped, dirty city for the countryside. Alice Williams's family lived in comfort away from the crowds of London.

The boys' father, James Williams, was a shopkeeper. Marrying him had dropped Alice a few steps down the social ladder. Still, Alice stayed friendly with her wealthy relatives. Roger was named for one of Alice's brothers.

Finally, Roger and his family returned to London. They lived on Long Lane, in a neighborhood called Smithfield. Crime was on the rise on Long Lane. The Williams family soon moved to Cow Lane, a better part of the neighborhood that attracted a higher class of customer for James's cloth business. James Williams had his shop in the front of the family's home.

People hurried about Cow Lane. Everyone was busy making, buying, or selling things. Roger took in all the sights and sounds: horses and coaches flashing by, pots and pans clinking, hammers ringing out. Sheep waiting for market day bleated in their pens. When the wind blew in his direction, Roger could smell them as well as hear them!

Come August, Cow Lane became more crowded than ever. For three days, St. Bartholomew's fair took over the neighborhood. People from all over England joined in the excitement. Traders, like James Williams, showed off their goods to hundreds of people a day. The open stall in front of the Williamses' shop brimmed with bolts of cloth.

Traffic was a big problem where Roger Williams grew up. A foreign visitor to 17th-century London wrote that carts "choke the streets so that a stranger . . . is happy if he escapes being crushed to pieces." There were speed limits and parking laws. A rider could not "Gallop his horse in the street." Nor could anyone "set any Carts in the Street by Night time." People who broke the city's traffic laws had to pay fines. If you did not drive your cart "patiently," you paid a fine of about 24 cents.

Helping out, Roger glanced beyond his father's stall. Jugglers, wrestlers, and actors performed for the crowds. He hoped his father would let him buy some gingerbread later.

Roger would have to watch out for pickpockets, though. Some came to the fair to steal, not to buy.

The fair was always over too soon. But there were still many interesting places in the neighborhood to explore. Smithfield had lots of bookstores. Roger wandered into them whenever he could. He'd been reading since he started school at age six.

School was held at a church. Besides reading, Roger studied religion at school. From six in the morning until four or five in the afternoon, Roger read aloud pages from the Bible. He memorized Bible verses, too.

Roger learned to read English as well as Latin, which was the language of trade everywhere in Europe. His father wanted Roger to learn Latin so that the boy could then work with many different customers at the Williamses' shop.

London was a big center of trade. From Cow Lane, Roger could see the tall masts of ships docked at London's port. On them, goods trav-

Roger first heard about John Smith and Pocahontas on Cow Lane, where neighbors talked about Smith's adventures in the New World.

eled all over the world. Some ships unloaded goods from England's Virginia colony.

At his church in Smithfield, Roger had seen the explorer Captain John Smith on visits home to England. On those days, talk around the neighborhood was all about Smith's adventures in Virginia. The story of his rescue by the Native American princess Pocahontas came to life when Pocahontas herself arrived in London. Roger was then about 13.

Roger was curious about people like Pocahontas. They lived in what was called a New World. What did the Bible say about them? His teachers didn't like to answer his questions about the Bible.

Roger thought it was boring to just memorize and read things aloud. He was learning something outside of class anyway, something called "secret writing." We know it today as "shorthand"–a way of shortening words to write them quickly. Roger learned shorthand to help him take notes of Sunday's **sermon** at church. On Mondays, teachers tested students on the sermon. Roger also wanted to learn shorthand because it might bring him work besides shopkeeping.

Sydrach, Roger's older brother, was in their father's line of work. Sydrach had a business shipping goods in and out of London. Roger's younger brother, Robert, planned to work for

Sydrach. But Roger wanted something else for himself.

Captain John Smith was not the only famous person who went to Roger's church. A very important lawyer named Sir Edward Coke worshiped there too. The story goes that one Sunday, Coke noticed Roger taking notes during the sermon. He called Roger over and asked to see his paper. The teenager's shorthand impressed him. He hired Roger to work for him as a clerk.

Coke was in his sixties but he still worked long hours. He expected his clerks to do the same. Roger's day began at 5:00 A.M. His duties included filing and copying legal papers. He also came up with questions to ask witnesses before a trial.

Trials took place at a building called Star Chamber. Looking up, you could see gold stars painted on the ceiling. Court was held on Wednesdays and Fridays. On those days, Roger joined Coke's other clerks at Star Chamber. There they recorded what happened at the day's trial. When he rose to speak, Coke turned to face his clerks seated against the wall. That way they could hear him more clearly and take better notes.

The audience at Star Chamber was always large. People filled the courtroom to listen to the lawyers argue their cases. Following the cases and watching the lawyers in action entertained the crowd. Coke strode about the courtroom in his robes. To stress an argument, he pointed or raised his fist.

Coke often defended the rights of the common person against the claims of the powerful. He once argued in court that the king could not seize a person's land or belongings, even in a time of war. As he put it, "every man's home is his castle."

From Coke, Roger learned that words could change people's minds. He also learned that law and government should protect people's rights. But often he saw they did not. In court, people were sentenced to punishment for their religious

Sir Edward Coke was a skillful and dramatic speaker, and Roger would listen intently as he recorded the arguments in shorthand for Coke.

beliefs. They might have their noses slit or faces burned with a branding iron.

These harsh punishments made Roger remember something he'd rather forget. Not far from his home in Smithfield, a man named Bartholomew Legate had been burned alive for speaking against church teachings.

At the time, England's government and church were practically the same. Laws dictated how people should practice religion. To worship any other way or hold different beliefs meant breaking the law, and lawbreakers faced certain punishment.

Threat of punishment didn't stop everyone from worshiping in their own way. Those who separated themselves from England's official church were called "Separatists." Among their secret meeting places were homes in Smithfield. Roger could thus put a familiar face on those punished for their beliefs. He may have played with their children. He may even have stumbled onto one of their meetings.

Roger later wrote that from the age of nine he was persecuted "in and out of my father's house." He was about nine when Bartholomew Legate was burned. He may have said something against this cruel act or spoken up for neighbors he saw dragged away to prison. Those who expressed sympathy for such people were under suspicion themselves. Roger's parents were concerned for his safety and tried to put out any spark of rebellion in him.

Like much of England's middle class, James and Alice Williams were Puritans. They wished to "purify" the Church of England. They wanted to make its practices fit their understanding of the Bible. Their goal was to reform, or change, the church but they would not go so far as to turn their backs on it or break the law doing so.

Still, Roger could not get out of his mind the suffering he'd seen. While working as a clerk to Edward Coke, Roger lived in Coke's home. Coke also believed that forcing people to act against their conscience was wrong. Roger and Coke became as close as a father and son. This relationship was to open up the future for Roger. Thanks to Coke, Roger was headed somewhere beyond the reach of most shopkeepers' sons.

As a young boy, Roger attended school at a church in Smithfield where he learned to read English and Latin. Later, Roger would be invited to attend the prestigious Charterhouse School.

2

Life Lessons

Charterhouse School stood less than a mile from Roger's home. But its hushed halls and restful gardens felt a long way from the crowds of Cow Lane. People at the school did not speak in English. They spoke in Latin.

The school was founded by Thomas Sutton, an educator who wanted to give working-class boys a chance to get ahead. Students who did well at Charterhouse went on to college.

At 18, Roger was older than most of his classmates at Charterhouse. His sponsor was Sir Edward Coke, who was a member of Charterhouse's governing board. He could easily ask the school to make exceptions. Coke paid for Roger's education and living costs, a sum that each year totaled more than the salary of many tradespeople in Smithfield.

All teaching at Charterhouse took place in a single room that held 40 students. Teachers roamed the classroom. They checked on each boy studying at his desk. One thing the boys wouldn't be studying was math—a subject that wasn't taught at the school. Someone at the time complained that Charterhouse students couldn't count the number of pages in their books.

The students always had their commonplace books somewhere nearby. These were notebooks in which Roger and his classmates copied down quotes and phrases from the Bible or other books approved by their teachers. These would usually be some very old books in Latin or Greek.

Students arranged quotes in their commonplace books under headings like "honor" or "wisdom." Roger turned to his commonplace book to prepare his writing assignments. His teachers were not interested in his personal experiences or opinions. Students at Charterhouse did not get good grades for being creative or original.

Older students such as Roger were expected to prepare speeches for special school events. One of these events was always Founder's Day, a time devoted to honoring Thomas Sutton. A teacher had to approve all speeches beforehand.

Thomas Sutton was the founder of the Charterhouse School, a place of learning where working-class boys could advance their education and prepare for college.

Roger spent two years at Charterhouse. In June 1623, he won a scholarship to attend Pembroke College at Cambridge University.

His classmates included sons of noblemen, called fellows. They were easy to spot in their large floppy hats, velvet jackets, boots, and spurs. They also had a way of getting around school bans on boating and playing cards. Other students, called sizers, paid very low fees and did work around the college.

Social differences kept these groups apart. At mealtime, the fellows sat around a table on a raised platform. Middle-class boys like Roger gathered at small tables placed against the walls, while sizers ate in the kitchen after they served the other students.

Roger's studies included philosophy, history, and grammar. Within the walls of Cambridge there was little talk of ideas shaking up science at the time. At Pembroke, as at Charterhouse, studies upheld the past.

Even the outcome of debates was no surprise. The debaters quoted from approved books and a school official decided the result. Real **controversy** was not allowed. In 1617, a student suggested debating whether to oppose a king who broke the law. The student was suspended.

Students who attended Cambridge University were not permitted to debate the laws of the king or to explore new ideas.

Roger later expressed disgust with life at Pembroke. He said it was foolish and empty. He ended up leaving the college before getting his master's degree. The degree would have assured him a comfortable living as a minister of the church. Why did he pass up this promising future?

As the religious leader of the Church of England, archbishop of Canterbury William Laud was insisting that everyone in the country follow his lead in religious matters. He and King Charles I were tightening their control over religion, forbidding any questioning of church teaching. At the same time, they made changes in the church's set of beliefs and practices. These changes swept away the independence of individual churches and ministers. For example, every minister had to lead worship dressed in a certain way. He had to wear a loose white gown over a long robe.

Roger felt strongly that people shouldn't be forced to worship any one way. "Forced worship stinks in God's Nostrils," he once said. However, graduates of Cambridge had to agree to the king and archbishop's changes. Roger could not bring himself to sign on the dotted line. "I desire not to sleep in security," he later wrote.

By early 1629, Roger was employed as a family chaplain at the manor home of Sir William

Masham in Essex County, outside of London. As chaplain he was responsible for the spiritual well-being of everyone at the manor. It was a seven-day-a-week job. The manor supplied almost all its own goods. Crews of people worked on the grounds, operating a dairy, bakery, and a room for dying fabrics. Workers also tended barns, fields, and orchards.

Archbishop Laud enforced strict obedience to the church, creating new beliefs and practices that every minister had to follow.

Roger's duties included leading prayers and giving sermons. He also read aloud from the Bible to Lady Masham and her helpers as they went about their chores. They might be busy making candles, tending bees, or canning cherries. In addition, Roger prayed personally with people at the manor. It was his job to guide them along spiritual paths.

Roger also carried messages for Masham to and from London. Masham counted on Roger's knowledge of the city. He also trusted Roger with letters and reports that spoke out against the king. The Masham manor was a political hot spot. Masham often met with other Puritan politicians. Most were members of **Parliament.**

Charles I and Parliament were bitter enemies. The king always seemed to need money. He insisted that Parliament raise taxes. Meanwhile, Parliament pressed for religious reform. Neither would give in to the other's demands. In 1629, their power struggle reached a breaking point. A stubborn king and equally stubborn Parliament faced off all winter.

When the showdown came in early March, Roger was in London. The king had lost all patience and was determined to do away with Parliament. When Roger returned to Essex, he was able to report that Parliament did not go without a fight.

The Puritans were far from defeated. Masham continued hosting political meetings at his home. Different plans of action were discussed.

At the Mashams', Roger heard talk of **colonies** in the New World that had been started by trading companies. Owners of the Massachusetts Bay Company included some of the wealthiest Puritans in England. They were eager to stake a claim in the rich trade opening up in America. Colonies in the New World also offered escape from the clutches of the Church of England.

One summer day in 1629, Roger was riding on horseback to a meeting on colonies in America. With him rode two Puritan ministers, John Cotton and Thomas Hooker. Roger found himself arguing with them. Archbishop Laud was demanding that all churches use an official prayer book. Cotton and Hooker said they used only the best prayers in the book. Roger, however, disagreed with any kind of official prayers.

Cotton and Hooker were just two of the Puritan leaders Roger was getting to know at the

Mashams'. He and the Puritans agreed on many things. For example, he believed as they did in careful study of the Bible. But his heart was stirred by more revolutionary aims. Only complete freedom of worship would satisfy him.

In addition, the wealthy Puritans clung to social differences and Roger had felt the sting of such differences at school. Now, he felt them again. Lady Masham's mother, Lady Joan Barrington, had a niece named Jane. Roger fell in love with Jane but his hopes were dashed by the proud Lady Barrington. She refused to allow her niece to marry a poor man with a dim future. After that, Roger became very ill.

Slowly, Roger regained his strength. He began paying attention to a personal maid of Lady Masham's daughter. Her name was Mary Barnard. On December 15, 1629, Roger and Mary were married. A year later, they prepared to set sail for Boston, a new settlement in the Massachusetts Bay Colony. Roger was ready to leave the Old World behind once and for all.

The Williamses' ship, the *Lyon,* was anchored at the English port of Bristol. There at the dock the couple met John Winthrop Jr., whose father was the governor of the Massachusetts Bay Colony. Governor Winthrop had ordered supplies rushed to the struggling Boston settlement. John was making sure all 200 tons of supplies were loaded on board the *Lyon.*

On December 1, 1630, the *Lyon* started off across the ocean. Stormy weather made it a difficult crossing. The ship tossed on rough seas. The passengers huddled in their cabins. Their discomfort lasted for a couple of months. A safe landing would make storms at sea just a memory for most of them. But for Roger and Mary, there would be many more storms ahead.

Roger and Mary Williams came to Boston in February 1631. Leaving behind the comforts of Masham manor, the Williamses began a new life in the wilderness of the New World. Like other colonists along the Atlantic coast, they learned new ways of farming better suited to the rocky soil.

Differing
Opinions

On February 9, 1631, the *Lyon* anchored in Boston **Harbor.** People onshore welcomed the ship and its supply of goods—tons of grain, butter, cheese, and lemons. These foodstuffs would see the starving colonists through until spring.

Roger and Mary had left the comforts of Masham manor far behind. They now lived on the edge of wilderness near Boston. "The air of the country is sharp, the rocks many," one settler complained, "the grass little, the winter cold, the summer hot, the gnats in summer biting, the wolves at night howling."

It seemed the harsh life in Boston had sent the town's preacher packing. Roger was offered his job. Such a chance did not come often to a young man under 30.

Roger's answer shocked everyone. He refused to serve "an unseparated people." Boston's church was too close to the Church of England for Roger's liking. He was disappointed to find church and state linked in the New World as in the Old. Here, too, a public whipping post punished breakers of church law.

Roger's refusal insulted Boston's leaders. In the spring, Roger and Mary moved north, to the settlement of Salem. Roger was invited to preach at the church there. The Massachusetts General Court—the governing body that laid down the law in the colony—demanded that the church take back its invitation. Shortly after that decision, Roger and Mary said good-bye to the settlement.

This time they headed south to Plymouth, a community that lay outside the control of the

Massachusetts Bay Colony and was settled by a Separatist group known as the Pilgrims. Roger was welcome to preach at their church.

Roger accepted no pay for his preaching. He learned to farm. He later wrote that he worked "hard at the hoe for my bread."

Roger also earned a living trading with the Native Americans. His brothers in England shipped goods, which were traded for the furs Roger bought from the natives. The natives bought things like pans, kettles, pins, needles, thread, toys, and tobacco.

Roger's trading took him throughout southern New England. He crisscrossed what are now the states of Massachusetts, Connecticut, and Rhode Island. He owned no horse. Instead he traveled by canoe. He also did a lot of walking.

On long trips, Roger stayed overnight with the native tribes. Under a blanket of bearskin, he slept in their tents. The tents were made of poles set in a circle and covered over with tree bark. With practice, Roger learned the natives'

Native Americans used wampum for money. They made wampum beads out of shells that they found along beaches or in clear, shallow pools. They cut and polished each shell until it gleamed and then pierced a hole in it. It was now a bead that could be strung together with other beads on a strip of plant stem. Strands of wampum beads were about six feet long. For trade with the colonists, a certain number of beads equaled a penny. This number changed depending on how much a penny bought in England.

language. They grew to mutually trust and respect each other.

Roger was finding it hard, however, to find a home among the English colonists. Even the people of Plymouth found him too extreme. By summer 1633, Roger and Mary were back in Salem.

Also that summer, the couple had their first child. They named her Mary. To support the family, Roger continued farming and trading with the Native Americans. He also found time to assist Reverend Samuel Skelton, the pastor at Salem's church.

When Skelton died in 1634, Salem's church chose Roger as pastor. His popularity grew. He believed that all people not trained as ministers, including women, had a right to speak up in church. Women speaking in church was unheard of in Boston.

Roger soon was in serious trouble with the Massachusetts General Court. He preached that the court had no right to punish people for breaking the Sabbath. People could be arrested, for example, for going fishing on Sundays.

Roger also argued against taking an oath agreeing to obey the laws of Massachusetts. He said it was wrong to call on the name of God to swear loyalty to a government of human beings. The Massachusetts General Court blamed Roger when some people refused to take the oath.

Roger upset the court, too, by urging colonists to "repent" of the "sin" of accepting land from England's king. He said the king used Christianity as an excuse for taking land from the Native Americans and giving it to the colonists. Roger insisted the native tribes had the same rights as people who called themselves

Christians. The colonists needed to pay the natives for use of their lands.

The Puritan leaders were furious. Roger struck at the principles at the very heart of their colony. They believed they were living on land promised to them as God's chosen people. Governor Winthrop said of Roger's protest: "If it be not treason, yet I dare say, it is strange boldness."

Roger was ordered to appear before the Massachusetts General Court. About this time, the court refused to consider Salem's claim to some nearby land because the people of Salem had made Roger their pastor without its approval. Meanwhile, Roger was pressuring his flock to separate from other New England churches. Salem's leaders chose instead to separate from Roger. The court suddenly agreed to Salem's claim.

When Roger stood before the court, he was on his own. Still, he refused to take back his statements. The next day, October 9, 1635, the court gathered to sentence him. In Boston's plain wooden meetinghouse, the judges and ministers sat together at a long table facing Roger. They accused him of spreading "dangerous opinions." He was ordered to leave Massachusetts Bay Colony within six weeks.

Later that month, Roger and Mary had a baby girl. Looking hopefully to the future, they named her Freeborn.

For now, Roger had to sell their house in Salem. He needed to buy supplies for building a new life in the

John Winthrop, governor of the Massachusetts Bay Colony, found Roger's radical ideas unsettling.

wilderness. At the same time, he became deathly ill and asked the court to allow him to stay until the following spring. The court gave in, but he was ordered to keep quiet about his opinions.

Roger could not keep silent. He continued preaching in his home. People were leaving

Salem's church to attend services at the Williamses'.

In January, the court ordered Roger to appear in Boston. He answered that he could not travel because of illness. He learned the court planned to ship him back to England.

The court sent a guard to Roger's home to arrest him. But Roger wasn't there. He'd fled into the wilderness three days before.

Roger had to make his way knee-deep in snow. He took shelter in caves and in the hollows of trees. He searched for dried berries and nuts to eat.

Roger was heading toward the village of the Wampanoags, a tribe that welcomed had the Pilgrims when they landed at Plymouth. They welcomed Roger, too.

Roger found himself in the middle of a disagreement between the Wampanoag and Narragansett tribes. They asked him to help settle the argument. The Narragansetts thanked him by giving him tribal lands to use. The Narragansetts

Roger Williams's experiences trading with the Native American tribes led to a mutual respect that enabled him to settle the argument between the Naragansetts and the Wampanoags.

were a powerful tribe in control of good land around Narragansett Bay.

The English claimed the lands of New England by right of discovery. People needed a **charter** from the king to settle the land. Roger instead made a deal with the Narragansetts. Canonicus and his nephew, Miantonomo, both led the tribe.

They demanded "not a penny," Roger said. Land use for the Native Americans had nothing to do with money. It had to do with friendship. "It was not price nor money that could have purchased Rhode Island," Roger later wrote. "Rhode Island was purchased by love."

But Roger wanted there to be no question about his right to the land. He paid the chiefs in gifts and favors. For example, he let them help themselves to his trading goods. (Canonicus often asked for sugar.) A **deed** was later written up proving Roger's payment for the land.

In the spring, Roger began to plant on land west of the Seekonk River. His family and several other **exiles** from New England joined him. Soon after planting, Roger got a letter from the governor of Plymouth Colony. The governor urged him to move to the other side of the river. Plymouth claimed the land to the west.

Roger and the others had to give up their harvest. They packed their canoes and paddled the Seekonk River. They followed a stream forming an arm of Narragansett Bay known as the Salt River. Sailing upriver, they sighted a neck of land jutting into the bay. They landed at a meadow cleared by the natives. Hills sheltered the clearing.

Thick forests covered the hills. Forests supplied wood for homes as well as turkeys and deer for food. Crops could be planted in the clearing below. Fresh springs crossed the meadow, and the rivers were full of fish. In addition, the surrounding bay offered a good harbor.

"And having in a Sense of God's merciful **providence** unto me," Roger later wrote, he called the place Providence. Roger started out seeking a place where he and his family could live in peace. He ended up founding a settlement for other seekers who made their way to America.

After crossing the Narragansett Bay in the
fall of 1636, Roger Williams met with the
Narragansett tribe to prevent a potential
uprising against the colonists.

4

Freedom for the Soul

In the fall of 1636, Roger crossed Narragansett Bay by canoe "through a stormy wind." He was heading for the Narragansetts' village. Talks were going on between the Narragansett and Pequot tribes. The Pequots were raiding English settlements. They wanted to unite Native Americans to fight the English. They were trying to talk the Narragansetts into joining them.

Massachusetts's governor asked Roger to meet with the Narragansetts. Roger was still banned from Massachusetts Bay Colony, but he put aside any bitterness he might be feeling. He hated the thought of bloodshed. So he agreed to speak up against the Pequots' war plans. During the talks, he slept in the same tent as the Pequot **representatives.** "I could not but nightly look for their bloody knives at my own throat," he wrote.

For three days and nights Roger argued for peace. Finally, the Narragansetts promised not to fight the English colonists. But Roger had more talking to do—and more traveling, too. He now had to convince another tribe, the Mohegans, not to join the Pequots.

That would not be easy. Uncas, the Mohegan chief, was jealous of the powerful Narragansett tribe. He just might join the Pequots. If the colonists were defeated, their Narragansett **allies** would be, too.

Roger managed to convince Uncas to stay friendly with the colonists. But he couldn't stop blood from being spilled. In the winter of 1637, war broke out between the Pequots and the New England colonies. The Mohegans and Narragansetts fought alongside the colonists.

Many of the English settlers had conflicts with the native tribes over land ownership. When war broke out between the Pequots and the colonists, Roger Williams was able to convince Uncas, the chief of the Mohegans, to remain friendly with the colonists.

The Narragansett chief, Miantonomo, set up camp outside Roger's home. With Miantonomo's help, Roger drew up a map of the Pequot region. The Pequot stronghold was Fort Mystic in southeastern Connecticut.

Roger sent a copy of the map to Massachusetts. He included a letter with the map. "[I]t would be pleasing to all natives, that women and children be spared," Roger wrote.

On the night of May 25, a surprise attack was made on Fort Mystic. The fort was set on fire. Roger's plea went ignored. About 700 Pequots died, women and children among them.

Roger protested the killings. "I fear some innocent blood cries at Connecticut," he wrote. Roger also protested selling the Pequot prisoners into slavery. He suggested instead they join other tribes. This followed Native American custom. Respecting native customs was only right, Roger argued.

The colonists won the Pequot War with the help of Mohegans and Narragansetts. Peace talks took place at Roger's house. Roger's home was always open to Native Americans. "One of Uncas' men, having hurt his foot, and disabled from travel" turned up at his door. Someone else who "took sick" on his way through Providence stayed until he was well.

The Williamses' home stood two stories high. The "fire room" rested on the ground floor. The family slept on the floor above. The family now included a son named Providence, who was born in 1638.

That same year, the population of the town of Providence totaled 85. Behind each home was a cornfield. Peas, oats, cabbage, and pumpkins grew in vegetable gardens. Goats were raised for milk and cheese. Pigs provided pork.

Town meetings took place every two weeks. Heads of households met and discussed common problems. Solutions were agreed upon by **majority** vote. People agreed, for example, to take turns guarding crops against wild animals. No one was denied a vote because of religion.

Roger himself did not belong to a church. He held services at his home on Sundays and several evenings a week. He called himself a "seeker."

More and more exiles from the Massachusetts Bay Colony were finding their way to Roger's door. Anne Hutchinson and her followers arrived in 1638. They believed people could worship God without a minister. This upset Massachusetts's government of ministers. They banned Hutchinson from the colony.

The Hutchinson group settled on Aquidneck Island in the Narragansett Bay. Roger helped Hutchinson make a fair deal with Canonicus and Miantonomo for the land. Hutchinson's settlement was called Portsmouth. It lay on the southern end of the island. A year later, a group of followers split off from Hutchinson. William Coddington led this group. They moved north to found a new settlement. They called their settlement Newport.

Newcomers to Providence were given the same amount of land as the early settlers. These

Anne Hutchinson was banished from the Massachusetts Bay Colony for her belief that people could worship God without a minister. Roger Williams helped Anne establish a settlement on Aquidneck Island.

early arrivals insisted on more land for themselves. Roger opened up land south of Providence for them. This land was included in Roger's deed with the Narragansett chiefs. It lay along the Pawtuxet River. The town of Pawtuxet was founded in 1638.

Also in 1638, Samuel Gorton and his followers arrived in Portsmouth. The Gortonites were suspicious of all government. Gorton's maid got into a hair-pulling fight with a neighboring woman. The woman's cow had wandered onto Gorton's property. Gorton argued with the judges throughout the trial. They were soon asked to leave Portsmouth.

Gorton stirred up trouble in Providence, too. One of his followers refused to pay a debt. Town representatives tried to take the man's cow as payment. Gortonites fought them off with pitchforks.

The Gortonites next moved to Pawtuxet. People there quickly became annoyed with them. Pawtuxet's leaders turned to Massachusetts Bay

Colony for help. Roger and other Narragansett Bay settlers were outraged. They feared Massachusetts would take over their lands.

The danger grew when Massachusetts joined with the three other New England colonies. In 1642, Massachusetts, Plymouth, Connecticut, and New Haven together formed the United Colonies. Providence and its neighboring settlements were not asked to join. They took this as a hint that the United Colonies meant to swallow them up. They would then no longer be free to worship as they chose.

Only by joining together themselves could the Narragansett Bay settlers face this threat. They needed to become a colony of their own. For this, they had to get a charter from England. A charter made them a legal settlement in English eyes. The United Colonies would then have to respect their borders.

The Narragansett Bay settlers chose Roger to represent them in London. They depended on him to convince the English government to give

Roger Williams's *A Key into the Language of America* was more than just a phrase book of the Narragansett language. It described how the Narragansett people lived, even providing details about their special kind of dry cereal, "which they eat with a little water, hot or cold." Williams was also surprised by how organized the tribe was. "I have traveled with near 200 of them at once, near 100 miles through the woods, every man carrying a little Basket of this at his back, and sometimes, in a hollow Leather [pack] about his middle [enough] for a man three or four days."

them a charter. In the spring of 1643, Roger set sail for London.

Onboard ship, Roger kept busy. He wrote a book called *A Key into the Language of America*. It listed about 2,500 Narragansett words and phrases and their meanings. At the same time, it painted a picture of the tribe's way of life. For example, the chapter "Of Traveling" mentions the "paths their naked hardened feet have made in the wilderness in most stony and rocky places."

When Roger arrived in England, he found a country in the grip of civil war. The struggle between Charles I and Parliament had moved to the battlefield. Soldiers were everywhere in London. A cannon guarded its gates.

Parliament was fighting for its life and it had little time to consider a charter. The king had fled London but still fought on. His army held control of several English towns, including Newcastle, a major coal mining area. That winter, London was not able to bring in coal to burn. People shivered with cold.

Roger's years in the wilderness taught him something about gathering wood. He led **volunteers** into London's nearby forests. The trees supplied wood for fuel.

Roger's popularity was on the rise. His book on the Narragansett language sold well. Londoners' interest in Native Americans had not died down since Pocahontas's visit years before.

Roger's powerful friends helped his cause. His old boss, Sir William Masham, introduced him to important members of Parliament. On March 14, 1644, Roger got his charter. It gave

How did Rhode Island get its name? Historians can't seem to agree. Some say Giovanni da Verrazano thought of the name. Verrazano was a European who explored the area in 1524. He described an island shaped like a triangle in the Narragansett Bay. He wrote that it reminded him of the island of Rhodes, near Turkey. Other historians say the name was thought of by Adriaen Block, a Dutch trader who visited the area in the 17th century. Noticing red clay along the island's shore, he called the place *Roodt Eylandt,* which means "Red Island" in Dutch.

the Narragansett Bay settlers the right to govern themselves. It also assured them freedom of religion.

Roger argued forcefully for this freedom in another book he wrote, titled *The Bloody Tenant of Persecution.* It appeared in London bookstores that summer. In its pages, Roger boldly stated the ideas on which his colony was built. He said that just as one size of shoe cannot fit every foot, a national church cannot fit every conscience.

The book caused an uproar. Religion was an explosive topic in England during the 1600s. On August 29, 1644, the city's hangman publicly burned Roger's book.

Roger was somewhere on the Atlantic Ocean at the time. He was heading back to America, charter in hand. Aquidneck Island and the lands around Narragansett Bay were now an English colony. Another name for Aquidneck Island was Rhode Island. The whole colony would be known by that name.

Roger returned to Providence on a well-worn path. Only eight years ago, he had not been able to find a single trail through these lands. Walking along the path, Roger caught sight of the Seekonk River. It was filled with canoes. The canoes carried friends and neighbors. They'd come to welcome Roger home.

Roger Williams's success in gaining a charter for Rhode Island from England's Parliament did not end the colonies' problems. Roger would have to return to England to defend the new colony against those who would challenge the charter.

Establishing a Colony

Rhode Island's charter did not magically unite the towns of Narragansett Bay. Roger had to travel from town to town and meet with people. He had to convince them to gather with representatives from other towns. Together they would plan a common government under the charter.

Finally, on May 18, 1647, the Narragansett Bay settlements held a meeting in Portsmouth. Representatives were sent by Portsmouth, Newport, Providence, and the new Gortonite settlement of Warwick. Roger led the group from Providence. He also led the meeting.

All the towns agreed to form a central government. "The form of Government," they stated, "is Democratical; that is to say, a Government held by the free and voluntary [agreement] of all." Every year, people in each town would elect two representatives to the colony's general assembly. This group would make laws for the colony.

Rhode Island's laws differed from those of other New England colonies. They didn't meddle in people's lives. Rhode Island had no laws, for example, forbidding certain people from wearing finery. Above all, people weren't punished for their beliefs. Also, very harsh punishments were done away with. In Rhode Island, a lawbreaker needn't fear part of his ear being cut off.

Still, all was not well. The new colony was suffering growing pains. For one thing, land fever was spreading through New England. Greedy settlers tried snatching up land in hopes of making money selling it later. Roger strongly opposed this idea. He believed newcomers should be able to get land at very little cost. Also, only landowners were allowed to vote. If new colonists could not buy land, Rhode Island could never be a true democracy.

William Harris was one of the settlers who had a bad case of land fever. He'd already demanded Roger deed him and other early settlers in Providence more land. Now he insisted the borders of that land went beyond the borders Roger laid out. The deed referred to the "town evidence," a piece of paper showing the land agreement Roger made with the Narragansetts.

Roger Williams traveled from town to town throughout Rhode Island to meet with people and convince them to join together and form a common government under a charter.

The Arnold family had a copy of the town evidence. William Arnold said his wife had used it to wrap seeds, then thrown it away. It ended up being torn and had to be pieced back together. The torn area happened to show the border being argued about. Harris took advantage of the confusion to press his claims.

Harris and the Arnold family were allies of Massachusetts Bay Colony. Massachusetts continued to hold onto Pawtuxet and also claimed part of Warwick. Massachusetts's leaders suffered from land fever, too. Rhode Island's charter didn't seem to matter to them.

Newport's William Coddington didn't care much about the charter either. Coddington never seemed to have enough power. Rhode Island's general assembly tried electing him president of the colony. Even this did not satisfy him. In January 1649, he set sail for England. He planned to make himself governor for life of Aquidneck Island. In April 1650 he succeeded.

Coddington's return from England in 1651 threw Rhode Island into chaos. Would the colony split in two? Did their charter still have meaning?

Roger would have to fight for the charter that

he had given life. In November 1651, he left for London. He sold his trading business to pay for the trip. This was a big risk. He now had six children to support. In addition, Roger had grown to love the wilderness. He'd miss his log hut in the shade of the forest.

Roger would not be traveling alone. At his side was John Clarke from Newport. Most people on Aquidneck Island opposed Coddington. They sent Clarke to speak for them.

It would not be easy to be heard. Parliament's attention was elsewhere. England faced war with the Dutch. Also, a struggle between Parliament and the army was brewing

Fortunately, Roger's friends held the majority in Parliament. Also, the head of the army was Masham's brother-in-law. Oliver Cromwell was then the most powerful person in England.

In October 1652, Coddington officially lost his governorship. Roger clearly showed Coddington's claim to Aquidneck Island to be false. But Rhode Island was still not safe.

Parliament hadn't yet moved to uphold Rhode Island's charter. The colonies of Plymouth and Connecticut, as well as Massachusetts, also laid claim to Narragansett lands. Representatives of Plymouth and Connecticut were in London to argue their case, too.

Meanwhile, upsetting news came from Rhode Island. Coddington was taking advantage of the uncertainty of the charter to hold onto power, and Harris and the Arnolds were winning people in Providence to their side. They claimed the town evidence showed they had more Narragansett land than Roger said they did. In 1653, competing general assemblies held elections. Each insisted it represented the colony.

Rhode Island desperately needed Roger's peacemaking skills. He left the future of the colony's charter in Clarke's able hands. In early summer of 1654, he arrived back in America.

Roger convinced his fellow colonists to meet and work out their differences together. Six representatives met from each town, with Roger in charge of running the meeting. On August 31, the four towns agreed to unite again under a single government. They called for a special election the following September.

At that election, Roger was voted president. Governing Rhode Island's people would not be easy. They were an independent-minded bunch. In addition, they were experimenting with a new kind of freedom. Roger was finding that experiments sometimes create or reveal new problems.

A big problem faced Roger not long after his election. In winter 1655, fighting broke out in Providence. A group of men were refusing to train for service in the **militia.** They pointed to their right to freedom of conscience. Their consciences, they said, told them serving in the militia was wrong. They would be willing to fight anyone who told them differently.

Roger saw this protest as a threat to the young, struggling colony. Freedom, he believed, must be balanced with responsibility. A free people were responsible for the well-being of their community.

Roger put his thoughts into words. He wrote a letter that was passed from town to town. He compared society to a ship at sea, its passengers sharing a common fate. They must cooperate or risk disorder and death.

Roger's letter quieted the protesters. Even after he stopped being president, Roger did his best to bring unity to Rhode Island. In 1658 he finally convinced Massachusetts to give up any claim to Rhode Island land. Pawtuxet then joined the colony. The year before, Coddington had agreed to cooperate with Rhode Island's elected government.

A new charter increased Rhode Island's confidence. In 1660 Charles II had become king of England. His government gave Rhode Island a new charter which upheld the freedoms of the old. Roger said their charter gave Rhode Islanders two "jewels": peace and liberty.

By 1660, Rhode Island's population totaled

about 1,500. The colony shocked the rest of New England by welcoming Jewish settlers. Roger himself visited them in their new home in Newport.

Quakers, or Friends, settled in Rhode Island, too. They urged believers to be guided by an "inner light" rather than by outside controls. This teaching upset leaders throughout the United Colonies. They punished the Friends harshly. They even demanded that Rhode Island ban Friends from its borders. However, Rhode Island refused to be bullied.

Despite pressure from the other colonies to ban Quakers from Rhode Island, the leaders of the new colony welcomed them.

The United Colonies, meanwhile, hoped to gobble up more and more Native American land. They'd already moved into Pequot holdings. To

Rhode Island's welcome of people of different faiths shocked the other colonies. They came up with insulting names for their new neighbor. Rhode Island was made fun of as "the Island of Error." People in Boston called Rhode Island "Rogue Island." A Connecticut minister referred to Rhode Island as the "sink" where the other colonies dumped their religious oddballs. New York ministers joked that Rhode Island was New England's "latrina" (The Latin word for "sewer"). They sneered that "all sorts of riff-raff" ended up there.

weaken the Narragansetts, they took advantage of tribal jealousies. When Uncas captured Miantonomo, they allowed him to kill the Narragansett chief.

At the same time, the United Colonies were making enemies with the new Wampanoag chief. His name was Metacomet, but he was also known as King Philip. He followed his older brother, Wamsutta, as chief. Metacomet blamed the colonists for his brother's death. Plymouth's leaders had ordered Wamsutta to appear before them. When he refused, they had seized him and marched him to Plymouth. He became sick with a fever, and on his way home, he died.

Metacomet was already angry with the colonists for taking tribal lands. Now he was angry enough to go to war. He set about uniting Native Americans against the colonists.

Metacomet had better luck than the Pequots had at stirring up hatred for the English. Miantonomo's death already turned the Narragansetts against them. Roger tried to talk the Narragansetts out of joining Metacomet. But his old friends, Canonicus and Miantonomo, were gone. The Narragansetts had a new chief, Canonchet. The young chief didn't trust the English at all. He would not promise to remain their ally.

King Philip's War began in June 1675. The Narragansetts' refusal to fight against Metacomet raised the suspicions of the United Colonies. In December, a colonial army marched through the snow to the Narragansett **stronghold.** They arrived on the 19th at the island village in what was known as the Great Swamp. They set the village on fire. Hundreds died, including women and children.

Canonchet's patience was at an end. Any peace agreement Canonicus and Miantonomo made with the English had lost its meaning. He led his warriors against their towns.

Rhode Island hadn't joined the other New England colonies in battle. Still, they readied themselves for attack. Roger served as captain of Providence's militia. News reached him that Pawtuxet and Warwick had been burned to the ground. He ordered Providence's women and children to the safety of Aquidneck Island.

In March 1676, Canonchet and his warriors reached Providence. Roger strode out to meet them. He was now in his seventies and walked with a cane. Leaning on his cane, he talked with Canonchet for over an hour. But Canonchet would not agree to leave the town in peace. Roger had been good to his people, though, and would not be harmed.

Roger's home was among those destroyed, along with the town's crops. The town records were saved, though. The town clerk threw the records from a window into a pond. He fished them out after the Narragansetts left.

Not long after, Canonchet was killed. In August 1676, Metacomet himself died at the colonists' hands. King Philip's War was over.

Roger now faced the task of helping rebuild Providence. He had served as Rhode Island's president for three terms. He had then filled a number of other offices in the colony. Now that he was older, he served

Metacomet (King Philip) blamed the colonists for his brother, Wamsutta's, death and sought revenge.

mostly in Providence. He led the town's first meeting after the war. The meeting was held under a large tree.

Sometime between January and March 1683, Roger Williams died. The people of Providence formed a procession in his honor. Guns were fired over his grave.

A spring flows near the area where Roger first landed in Providence. The spot is clearly marked with a sign that invites people "to fetch water at this spring forever." Roger's own example shines clear. He showed the way for treating Native Americans with respect. And his colony's separation of church and state became a model for the United States government. To this day, Roger Williams remains a source of inspiration for defenders of freedom everywhere.

GLOSSARY

ally a helper or partner

charter an official paper creating a new state or city

colony a settlement tied by law to a parent country

controversy difference of opinion so strong it can be upsetting

deed a legal paper having to do with owning land or goods

exile a person forced to leave his or her country or home

harbor deep water alongside land where it's safe for ships to anchor

majority a greater number

militia a group fighting in defense of a community

Parliament England's lawmaking body

providence the guidance and care of a higher power

representative a person speaking for a group

sermon a speech given as part of a worship service

stronghold a place where a group of people feel safe and protected

volunteer a person who offers to do something

CHRONOLOGY

1603 Roger Williams is born in London.

1623 Admitted to Cambridge University on June 29.

1629 Becomes chaplain at the manor home of Sir William Masham; marries Mary Barnard on December 15.

1630 Sails to New England with Mary aboard the *Lyon* on December 1; arrives at Boston Harbor the following February.

1635 Ordered to leave Massachusetts Bay Colony on October 9.

1636 Flees Salem for Narragansett Bay in January to escape being sent back to England; begins settlement at Providence in early summer.

1637 Holds peace talks in his home, ending the Pequot War.

1643 Sets sail for England to get charter for new colony; begins writing *A Key into the Language of America* while onboard ship.

1644 Receives a charter for the colony of Rhode Island from English Parliament on March 14; his book, *The Bloody Tenant of Persecution* burned publicly in London that summer.

1651 Travels to England to defend Rhode Island's charter.

1654 Elected president of Rhode Island on September 12.

1657 Retires from presidency after three terms; continues to serve in different government posts.

1676 Providence home burned down in King Philip's War.

1683 Roger Williams dies in late winter in Providence.

COLONIAL TIME LINE

1607 Jamestown, Virginia, is settled by the English.

1620 Pilgrims on the *Mayflower* land at Plymouth, Massachusetts.

1623 The Dutch settle New Netherlands, the colony that later becomes New York.

1630 Massachusetts Bay Colony is started.

1634 Maryland is settled as a Roman Catholic colony. Later Maryland becomes a safe place for people with different religious beliefs.

1636 Roger Williams is thrown out of the Massachusetts Bay Colony. He settles Rhode Island, the first colony to give people freedom of religion.

1682 William Penn forms the colony of Pennsylvania.

1688 Pennsylvania Quakers make the first formal protest against slavery.

1692 Trials for witchcraft are held in Salem, Massachusetts.

1712 Slaves revolt in New York. Twenty-one blacks are killed as punishment.

1720 Major smallpox outbreak occurs in Boston. Cotton Mather and some doctors try a new treatment. Many people think the new treatment shouldn't be used.

1754 French and Indian War begins. It ends nine years later.

1761 Benjamin Banneker builds a wooden clock that keeps precise time.

1765 Britain passes the Stamp Act. Violent protests break out in the colonies. The Stamp Act is ended the next year.

1775 The battles of Lexington and Concord begin the American Revolution.

1776 Declaration of Independence is signed.

FURTHER READING

Avi. *Finding Providence: The Story of Roger Williams*. New York: Harper Trophy, 1997.

Barrett, Tracy. *Growing Up in Colonial America*. Brookfield, CT.: Millbrook Press, 1995.

Fradin, Dennis B. *The Rhode Island Colony*. Chicago: Children's Press, 1989.

Maestro, Betsy. *The New Americans: Colonial Times, 1620–1689*. New York: Lothrop, Lee & Shepard Books, 1998.

Washburn, Carolyn Kott. *A Multicultural Portrait of Colonial Life*. New York: Marshall Cavendish, 1994.

INDEX

INDEX

PICTURE CREDITS

ABOUT THE AUTHOR

AMY ALLISON first wrote a paper on Roger Williams when she was a student at Rosemary Hills Elementary School in Silver Spring, Maryland. She now lives in the Los Angeles area, where she works as a writer and editor. Her poetry has appeared in *Cricket* magazine. Her other books include *Shakespeare's Globe* and *Gargoyles on Guard*.

Senior Consulting Editor **ARTHUR M. SCHLESINGER, JR.** is the leading American historian of our time. He won the Pulitzer Prize for his book *The Age of Jackson* (1945) and again for *A Thousand Days* (1965). This chronicle of the Kennedy Administration also won a National Book Award. He has written many other books including a multi-volume series, *The Age of Roosevelt*. Professor Schlesinger is the Albert Schweitzer Professor of the Humanities at the City University of New York, and has been involved in several other Chelsea House projects, including the REVOLUTIONARY WAR LEADERS biographies on the most prominent figures of early American history.